HASHIM(
THYROIDITIS
RECIPES COOKBOOK

20 Savory and Wholesome
Autoimmune Protocol (AIP) Diets to
Support the Thyroid Gland

Yvette Johnson

Table of Contents

Introduction

In a world where a healthy metabolism, hormone balance, and body temperature are all dependent on the thyroid gland, there is a disorder known as Hashimoto's thyroiditis. This condition develops when the thyroid is unable to perform at its peak due to persistent inflammation.

We come across individuals who are struggling with Hashimoto's symptoms. They struggle with constipation, weight gain, dry skin, hair loss, weariness, and an unpleasant sensitivity to cold on a regular basis. They seek a solution, but their hope wavers.

They find a marvelous cookbook—a source of comfort and nourishment—while searching for respite. Its pages reveal a veritable gold mine of nutritious meals created especially for the Autoimmune Protocol (AIP) diet. Embracing the power of nutrient-dense goods and doing away with possible triggers, they set out on their culinary expedition with cautious hope.

Their bodies react as they relish each flavorful mouthful. An increased vigor takes its place as the inflammation fades. They achieve balance with their weight, get their radiance back, and make energy their constant companion. With the help of this cookbook, they learn about the deep potential of the AIP diet to lessen the stifling symptoms of Hashimoto's thyroiditis.

Together, they embark on this life-changing adventure, feeding their bodies and taking back control of their lives one nutritious meal at a time.

Savory and Wholesome Autoimmune Protocol (AIP) Recipes

1. Baked Salmon with Roasted Brussels Sprouts:

Ingredients:

- 4 oz. salmon filet
- Brussels sprouts
- Olive oil
- Lemon juice
- Garlic powder
- Salt and pepper

Instructions:

1. Preheat the oven to 400°F (200°C).
2. Line a baking sheet with parchment paper, then place the salmon filet on it.
3. Toss the Brussels sprouts with olive oil, lemon juice, garlic powder, salt, and pepper.
4. Spread the Brussels sprouts around the salmon.

5. Bake for 15-20 minutes, or until the salmon is cooked through and the Brussels sprouts are tender.

2. Turkey and Vegetable Stir-Fry:

Ingredients:

- 4 oz ground turkey
- Assorted vegetables (e.g., zucchini, carrots, bell peppers)
- Coconut aminos (a soy sauce alternative)
- Garlic, minced
- Ginger, grated
- Coconut oil
- Salt and pepper

Instructions:

1. Heat coconut oil in a pan or wok over medium heat.
2. Add and cook the ground turkey until it becomes brown.
3. Add the minced garlic and grated ginger, and stir for another minute.

4. Add the assorted vegetables and stir-fry until tender.
5. Season with coconut aminos, salt, and pepper. Stir well.
6. Serve hot over cauliflower rice or steamed vegetables.

3. Chicken and Vegetable Soup:

Ingredients:

- 4 oz. chicken breast, cooked and shredded
- Assorted vegetables (e.g., carrots, celery, onions)
- Chicken broth (homemade or low-sodium)
- Fresh herbs (such as thyme or parsley)
- Olive oil
- Salt and pepper

Instructions:

1. Heat the olive oil in a large pot.

2. Add the vegetables and sauté until they start to soften.
3. Pour in the chicken broth and boil it.
4. Add the shredded chicken and fresh herbs.
5. Cover the pot, decrease the heat, and simmer for about 15–20 minutes.
6. Season with salt and pepper to taste.
7. Serve it hot as a comforting and nourishing soup.

4. Zucchini Noodles with Bolognese Sauce

Ingredients:

- 2 medium zucchinis, spiralized into noodles
- Ground beef or turkey
- Onion, diced
- Garlic, minced
- Canned crushed tomatoes
- Tomato paste
- Italian seasoning
- Olive oil
- Salt and pepper

Instructions:

1. Heat the olive oil in a skillet on moderate heat.
2. Add the ground beef or turkey, diced onion, and minced garlic. Cook until browned.
3. Stir in the crushed tomatoes, tomato paste, and Italian seasoning.
4. Simmer for 10–15 minutes to let the flavors meld together.
5. In a separate skillet, sauté the zucchini noodles in olive oil until tender.
6. Season the Bolognese sauce with salt and pepper to taste.
7. Serve the zucchini noodles topped with the Bolognese sauce.

5. Grilled Chicken with Cauliflower Mash and Steamed Broccoli

Ingredients:

- 4 oz. chicken breast, grilled
- Cauliflower, cut into florets
- Garlic, minced
- Dairy-free milk (such as coconut milk or almond milk)

- Ghee (clarified butter) or coconut oil
- Broccoli florets
- Lemon juice
- Salt and pepper

Instructions:

1. Grill the chicken breast until cooked through.
2. In a pot of boiling water, cook the cauliflower until tender. Drain.
3. In a blender or food processor, blend the cooked cauliflower, minced garlic, dairy-free milk, and ghee or coconut oil until smooth and creamy.
4. Steam the broccoli florets until tender-crisp. Combine with salt, pepper and lemon juice.
5. Serve the grilled chicken with a side of cauliflower mash and steamed broccoli.

6. Roasted Turkey Breast with Sweet Potato Mash and Sautéed Kale:

Ingredients:

- 4 oz. turkey breast, roasted
- Sweet potato, peeled and cubed
- Coconut oil
- Coconut milk
- Cinnamon
- Kale leaves
- Garlic, minced
- Lemon juice
- Salt and pepper

Instructions:

1. Roast the turkey breast until cooked through.
2. Steam or boil the sweet potato cubes until soft. Drain.
3. In a bowl, mash the sweet potatoes with coconut oil, coconut milk, and a sprinkle of cinnamon.
4. In a separate pan, heat coconut oil over medium heat. Put the minced garlic, then sauté for one minute.
5. Add the kale leaves and sauté until wilted. Drizzle salt, pepper, and lemon juice on it.
6. Serve the roasted turkey breast with a side of sweet potato mash and sautéed kale.

7. Beef Stir-Fry with Coconut Cauliflower Rice:

Ingredients:

- 4 oz. beef sirloin, thinly sliced
- Cauliflower, grated or processed into a rice-like texture
- Coconut aminos
- Ginger, grated
- Garlic, minced
- Coconut oil
- Assorted vegetables (e.g., broccoli, bell peppers, snap peas)
- Green onions, chopped
- Salt and pepper

Instructions:

1. In a bowl, marinate the sliced beef with coconut aminos, grated ginger, minced garlic, salt, and pepper. Set aside for 15 minutes.
2. Heat the coconut oil in a pan or wok.
3. Add the marinated beef and cook until it turns brown.
4. Add the assorted vegetables and stir-fry until tender-crisp.

5. In a separate pan, sauté the grated cauliflower in coconut oil until cooked but still slightly crunchy.
6. Season the beef stir-fry with coconut aminos, salt, and pepper.
7. Serve the beef stir-fry over coconut cauliflower rice, garnished with chopped green onions.

8. Salmon and Avocado Nori Rolls:

Ingredients:

- 4 oz. cooked salmon, flaked
- Nori seaweed sheets
- Avocado, sliced
- Cucumber, julienned
- Carrot, julienned
- Coconut aminos (for dipping sauce)
- Wasabi and pickled ginger (optional)
- Sesame seeds (optional)

Instructions:

1. Lay a sheet of nori seaweed on a bamboo sushi mat or a flat surface.

2. Spread a thin layer of flaked salmon on the nori sheet, leaving some space at the edges.
3. Arrange slices of avocado, julienned cucumber, and julienned carrot on top of the salmon.
4. Roll the nori tightly using the sushi mat or your hands, applying gentle pressure to keep the ingredients together.
5. Slice the roll into bite-sized pieces.
6. Repeat with the remaining ingredients.
7. Serve the salmon and avocado nori rolls with coconut aminos for dipping and, optionally, with wasabi, pickled ginger, and sesame seeds.

9. Chicken and Vegetable Curry with Cauliflower Rice:

Ingredients:

- 4 oz. chicken breast, diced
- Cauliflower, grated or processed into a rice-like texture
- Onion, diced
- Garlic, minced

- Curry powder
- Coconut milk
- Assorted vegetables (e.g., bell peppers, zucchini, and carrots)
- Coconut oil
- Fresh cilantro, chopped
- Salt and pepper

Instructions:

1. Heat the coconut oil over moderate heat in a skillet
2. Put the diced chicken, cook until it turns brown.
3. Remove the chicken from the skillet and set it aside.
4. In the same skillet, add diced onion and minced garlic. Sauté until translucent.
5. Put curry powder and stir for about one minute.
6. Put in the coconut milk and simmer.
7. Add the assorted vegetables and cooked chicken back to the skillet. Cook until the vegetables are tender.
8. In a separate pan, sauté the grated cauliflower in coconut oil until cooked but still slightly crunchy.

9. Season the curry with salt and pepper. Garnish with chopped cilantro.
10. Serve the chicken and vegetable curry over cauliflower rice.

10. Turkey Lettuce Wraps:

Ingredients:

- 4 oz. ground turkey
- Lettuce leaves (such as butter lettuce or romaine lettuce)
- Carrot, grated
- Cucumber, julienned
- Fresh mint leaves
- Fresh cilantro leaves
- Lime juice
- Coconut aminos (for dipping sauce)
- Salt and pepper

Instructions:

1. Cook the ground turkey in a skillet until it becomes brown. Season with salt and pepper.
2. Arrange lettuce leaves on a plate.

3. Fill each lettuce leaf with a spoonful of cooked ground turkey.
4. Top with grated carrot, julienned cucumber, mint leaves, and cilantro leaves.
5. Drizzle with lime juice and coconut aminos.
6. Roll up the lettuce leaves to create wraps.
7. Serve the turkey lettuce wraps with additional coconut aminos for dipping.

11. Beef and Broccoli Stir-Fry:

Ingredients:

- 4 oz. beef sirloin, thinly sliced
- Broccoli florets
- Coconut aminos
- Ginger, grated
- Garlic, minced
- Coconut oil
- Green onions, chopped
- Sesame oil
- Sesame seeds
- Salt and pepper

Instructions:

1. In a bowl, marinate the sliced beef with coconut aminos, grated ginger, minced garlic, salt, and pepper. Set aside for 15 minutes.
2. In a pan or wok, warm coconut oil over medium heat.
3. Add the meat that has been marinated, and heat it until it is browned.
4. Broccoli florets should be added and stir-fried until tender-crisp.
5. Season with coconut aminos, sesame oil, salt, and pepper.
6. Add sesame seeds and finely chopped green onions as a garnish.
7. Serve the beef and broccoli stir-fry over cauliflower rice or zucchini noodles.

12. Herb-Roasted Chicken Thighs with Steamed Asparagus

Ingredients:

- 2 chicken thighs, bone-in and skin-on

- Fresh herbs (such as rosemary, thyme, or sage), chopped
- Garlic, minced
- Lemon zest
- Olive oil
- Salt and pepper
- Asparagus spears

Instructions:

1. Preheat the oven to 400°F (200°C).
2. In a small bowl, combine chopped fresh herbs, minced garlic, lemon zest, olive oil, salt, and pepper to make a marinade.
3. Rub the chicken thighs with the marinade, ensuring it coats both sides.
4. Place the chicken thighs on a baking sheet lined with parchment paper, skin-side up.
5. Roast in the preheated oven for 30–35 minutes, or until the chicken is cooked through and the skin is crispy.
6. While the chicken is roasting, steam the asparagus spears until tender.

7. Serve the herb-roasted chicken thighs with steamed asparagus.

13. Tuna Salad Lettuce Wraps:

Ingredients:

- 4 oz. canned tuna, drained
- Paleo mayo (or mashed avocado for a dairy-free option)
- Red onion, diced
- Celery, diced
- Dill pickle, diced
- Fresh dill, chopped
- Lettuce leaves
- Lemon juice
- Salt and pepper

Instructions:

1. In a bowl, combine canned tuna, Paleo mayo (or mashed avocado), diced red onion, diced celery, diced dill pickle, chopped fresh dill, lemon juice, salt, and pepper. Mix well.
2. Lay lettuce leaves on a plate.
3. Spoon the tuna salad onto each lettuce leaf.

4. Wrap the lettuce leaves around the tuna salad to create wraps.
5. Serve the tuna salad lettuce wraps as a light and refreshing meal.

14. Baked Cod with Roasted Root Vegetables:

Ingredients:

- 4 oz. cod filet
- Assorted root vegetables (such as carrots, parsnips, and sweet potatoes), peeled and chopped
- Fresh thyme leaves
- Garlic, minced
- Lemon zest
- Olive oil
- Salt and pepper

Instructions:

1. Preheat the oven to 400°F (200°C).
2. Place the cod filet on a baking sheet lined with parchment paper.
3. In a bowl, toss the chopped root vegetables with fresh thyme leaves,

minced garlic, lemon zest, olive oil, salt, and pepper.

4. Spread the seasoned root vegetables around the cod filet.
5. Bake for 15–20 minutes, or until the cod is cooked through and the root vegetables are tender.
6. Serve the baked cod with roasted root vegetables.

15. Spinach and Mushroom Omelette:

Ingredients:

- 3 eggs
- Spinach leaves
- Mushrooms, sliced
- Onion, diced
- Garlic, minced
- Coconut oil
- Salt and pepper

Instructions:

1. Whisk the eggs with salt and pepper thoroughly.

2. Heat the coconut oil in a skillet over moderate heat.
3. Add the diced onion and minced garlic. Sauté until translucent.
4. Sauté the mushrooms until the liquid is released after adding the thinly sliced mushrooms.
5. Add the spinach leaves and stir until wilted.
6. Pour the whisked eggs into the skillet, swirling to distribute the vegetables evenly.
7. Cook the omelet until the edges are set and the center is slightly runny.
8. Cook the omelet for another minute after folding it in half.
9. Serve the spinach and mushroom omelet as a nutrient-packed breakfast or light meal.

16. Baked Chicken Drumsticks with Mashed Butternut Squash:

Ingredients:

- 2 chicken drumsticks
- Butternut squash, peeled, seeded, and cubed

- Coconut oil
- Nutmeg
- Cinnamon
- Coconut milk
- Fresh parsley, chopped
- Salt and pepper

Instructions:

1. Preheat the oven to 400°F (200°C).
2. Lined the baking sheet with parchment paper, and arrange the chicken drumsticks on it.
3. Rub the drumsticks with coconut oil and season with salt and pepper.
4. Bake for 40–45 minutes, or until the chicken is cooked through and the skin is crispy.
5. Meanwhile, steam or boil the cubed butternut squash until soft. Drain.
6. In a bowl, mash the butternut squash with coconut oil, a sprinkle of nutmeg and cinnamon, coconut milk, salt, and pepper.
7. Serve the baked chicken drumsticks with a side of mashed butternut squash, garnished with fresh parsley.

17. Beef and Cabbage Stir-Fry:

Ingredients:

- 4 oz. beef sirloin, thinly sliced
- Green cabbage, shredded
- Carrot, julienned
- Coconut aminos
- Ginger, grated
- Garlic, minced
- Coconut oil
- Green onions, chopped
- Salt and pepper

Instructions:

1. In a bowl, marinate the sliced beef with coconut aminos, grated ginger, minced garlic, salt, and pepper. Set aside for 15 minutes.
2. Heat coconut oil in a pan or wok over medium heat.
3. Add the marinated beef and cook until browned.
4. Add the shredded cabbage and julienned carrot. Stir-fry until the vegetables are tender-crisp.

5. Season with coconut aminos, salt, and pepper.
6. Garnish with chopped green onions.
7. Serve the beef and cabbage stir-fry as a flavorful and nourishing meal.

18. Stuffed Bell Peppers:

Ingredients:

- Bell peppers (any color), halved, and seeds removed
- Ground turkey or beef
- Onion, diced
- Garlic, minced
- Spinach leaves, chopped
- Tomato sauce (sugar-free)
- Italian seasoning
- Olive oil
- Salt and pepper

Instructions:

1. Preheat the oven to 375°F (190°C).
2. Heat the olive oil in a skillet.
3. Add the ground turkey or beef, diced onion, and minced garlic. Cook until browned.

4. Add the chopped spinach leaves and sauté until wilted.
5. Stir in the tomato sauce and Italian seasoning. Season with salt and pepper.
6. Spoon the mixture into the halved bell peppers, filling them completely.
7. Place the stuffed bell peppers on a baking dish lined with parchment paper.
8. Bake for 25–30 minutes, or until the peppers are tender and the filling is cooked through.
9. Serve the stuffed bell peppers as a satisfying and nutrient-dense meal.

19. Grilled Shrimp Skewers with Zucchini and Red Onion:

Ingredients:

- Shrimp, peeled and deveined
- Zucchini, sliced into rounds
- Red onion, cut into chunks
- Fresh lemon juice
- Garlic powder
- Paprika
- Olive oil

- Salt and pepper

Instructions:

1. Preheat the grill to medium heat.
2. In a bowl, toss the shrimp, zucchini rounds, and red onion chunks with fresh lemon juice, garlic powder, paprika, olive oil, salt, and pepper.
3. Thread the shrimp, zucchini, and red onion onto skewers.
4. Grill the skewers for three-four minutes on each side, or until the shrimp turns pink and properly cooked.
5. Serve the grilled shrimp skewers with a squeeze of lemon juice.

20. Roasted Vegetable Medley:

Ingredients:

- Assorted vegetables (such as carrots, parsnips, beets, and Brussels sprouts), peeled and chopped
- Fresh herbs, chopped (e.g thyme or rosemary)
- Garlic, minced

- Olive oil
- Balsamic vinegar
- Salt and pepper

Instructions:

1. Preheat the oven to 400°F (200°C).
2. In a large mixing bowl, toss the chopped vegetables with chopped fresh herbs, minced garlic, olive oil, balsamic vinegar, salt, and pepper.
3. Spread the seasoned vegetables in a single layer on a baking sheet lined with parchment paper.
4. Roast in the preheated oven for 25–30 minutes, or until the vegetables are tender and caramelized.
5. Serve the roasted vegetable medley as a delicious and nutritious side dish.

Conclusion

Enjoy these savory and wholesome recipes that support the thyroid gland and are suitable for the Autoimmune Protocol (AIP) diet! Remember to check for any specific dietary restrictions or allergies before preparing these recipes.

Printed in Great Britain
by Amazon

26573644R00020